A House By Itself

T0151630

A House By Itself

Selected Haiku: Masaoka Shiki

Translated by John Brandi
and Noriko Kawasaki Martinez

WHITE PINE PRESS / BUFFALO, NEW YORK

White Pine Press
P.O. Box 236
Buffalo, New York 14201

Publication of this book was made possible, in part, by the
support of the Witter Bynner Foundation for Poetry and with
public funds from the New York State Council on the Arts,
with the support of Governor Andrew M. Cuomo and the
New York State Legislature, a State Agency.

Cover image copyright © 2017 by John Brandi

First Edition

Printed and bound in the United States of America.

ISBN: 978-1-945680-09-0

Library of Congress Control Number: 2016960876

CONTENTS

A House By Itself

Masaoka Shiki: His Life and Legacy

Charles Trumbull

Masaoka Shiki was in the right place at just the right time. He was born just as Japan was being "opened" to the West. With the demise of the Tokugawa shogunate and the ascension of the Meiji emperor, a country that had been insular for centuries began a rapid modernization. The air was full to the brim with radically new ideas. A cousin of Shiki's described the tenor of the times: "We reached adolescence just after the dissolution of the feudal system. All had been sown afresh. But while the old order had fallen, nothing new had yet been created in its place." (Beichman 8)

The crosscurrent of influences from the West was both official and informal. The Japanese government enthusiastically embraced Western economic and social institutions, including even aspects of culture and literature. Individual artists and writers on their own initiative rushed to steep themselves in Western culture and aesthetics. Shiki was resolved to step into that cultural vortex. He was so successful in providing a new framework for the old poetic genres of *hokku* and *haikai* (which he renamed "haiku") and *waka* (now "tanka") such that his ideas—or reactions to them—have dominated Japanese poetic theory ever since.

Shiki's Life

Shiki was born as Masaoka Tsunenori into a low-ranking samurai family on September 17, 1867, in Matsuyama on the southern Japanese island of Shikoku. A sister, Ritsu, was born three years later. His father, an alcoholic, died when the boy was five. Shiki started grade school in 1873, and at the same time he began study of the Chinese classics with his grandfather, a stern teacher in the old-fashioned mode, and soon became proficient in reading and writing Chinese poetry.

In 1880, at age thirteen, he coughed blood for the first time and was diagnosed with tuberculosis. Young Tsunenori took the pen name "Shiki," one name for the *hototogisu*, a kind of cuckoo that was believed to sing with such gusto that it would spit up blood doing so.

> Farther and farther away
> go the lanterns—
> the *hototogisu*'s call

In 1883 Shiki left the middle school in Matsuyama, went to Tokyo to live with an uncle and enroll in school there. The following year he passed the entrance exam for the University Preparatory School. At this time his main interest was radical politics. Shiki was never a dedicated student, and the following year he failed his school exams. He changed his career goals to philosopher, and soon after he discovered the discipline of aesthetics, read Herbert Spencer's *On Style*, and decided that this field would be his life's work.

Shiki graduated from the Higher Middle School in 1890 and entered the Imperial University in the Japanese literature department. By the spring of 1891, however, his interest in formal education and philosophy was flagging, and he skipped his final university examinations.

Shiki's first haiku date from 1885. By 1892 he was actively writing literary criticism, and he undertook an independent examination of the history of *haikai* and *waka*, and, having completed his study, began his reform of haiku. He left the university and took a position as haiku editor of *Nippon*. In that newspaper he published editorials, which included his criticism—controversial to the point of scandal—of haiku icon Matsuo Bashō and praise for Yosa Buson, a painter-poet whose work had fallen into shadow. Shiki's development of the aesthetic of *shasei*—sketching from life—also dates to these years.

In 1895, with his typical impulsiveness, Shiki decided he must go to China, where Japan was waging war, as a correspondent. The conflict was soon over, however, and Shiki never reached the front. He was shipped back home, suffered a lung hemorrhage from his tuberculosis, and was hospitalized in Kobe. He was not expected to live but somehow pulled through. He returned to Matsuyama and stayed to recuperate with his friend Natsume Sōseki, a student of English literature and soon to become a great novelist.

The last decade of Shiki's life were amazingly productive and volatile; he changed directions frequently. In his last ten years Shiki composed more than 90% of his more than 25,000 haiku as well as thousands of tanka, and two journals.

The haiku journal *Hototogisu* began publication in Matsuyama in 1897 under Shiki's aegis. He could not edit it himself because of his illness, so he named his close friend Takahama Kyoshi, to look after it. Shiki and Kyoshi took Hototogisu with them when they moved to Tokyo. There Shiki underwent surgery for his illness, but his medical condition continued to worsen. From 1897 onward he was completely bedridden, suffering excruciating back pain, fever, and festering tubercular boils. Despite his condition—or perhaps because he felt driven to complete his life work—in 1898 Shiki additionally undertook a reform of tanka.

By 1901 he required constant medical care, which was provided by his sister and mother. Despite his dire condition, Shiki continued his literary work and brush painting, and still enjoyed visiting with his many friends. On the evening of September 19, 1902, he died in Tokyo. Scant hours earlier he had managed to write three last haiku in his own hand.

SHIKI'S ART

Shiki's greatest achievement was his resuscitation of haiku as a poetic genre. Along the way he came up with the novel notion of "Japanese literature," placing poetry, drama, and novels, as well as *haikai* and *waka*, under a single rubric for the first time. Periodically, from the time of the origins of haiku in the 15th century, haiku would decline into triviality. In turn each of the four pillars of classical Japanese haiku—Bashō, Chiyo-ni, Buson, and Issa—had taken it upon themselves to restore the integrity of the genre. Shiki did the same, but more rigorously and formally.

His great contribution to haiku was *shasei,* or "sketching from life," this in contradistinction to the prevalent subjective, imaginative, even fanciful approach to composition. Although a thread of the idea of that art should hew close to life can be traced through earlier Japanese literature and back even to Chinese poetry, Shiki's inspiration clearly came from Western philosophy, aesthetics, and painting. The term *shasei* had earlier been used in Japan for the English "sketch" and French "dessin"; Shiki now applied it to haiku.

Shiki's milieu in Tokyo included a group of young painters, foremost among them Nakamura Fusetsu, who was working in the European style: "The basic method of Western painting is first, correct form, second, balance of color, and third, to always imagine as you paint that you are looking at a beautiful scene through a window" (Beichman 54–55). Fusetsu's paintings are remarkable for their realism, featuring perspective, subtlety of color, and absence of the stylization characteristic of classical Japanese styles. Shiki's thinking was catalyzed by the idea of representing what was true to life and nature and not prettified with the author's fancy or poetic imagination. Most important was fidelity of the poet to Nature, i.e., reality. To be shunned was empty imagination divorced from observable reality.

After some time, however, Shiki came to realize that strict sketching from life can devolve into arid description that does not attain the goal in haiku of poetic truth. Shiki postulated a stage aesthetically higher than but organically evolved from *shasei* that he called "selective realism." Haiku scholar Makoto Ueda (12–13) notes that in selective realism, "the selection [is] made by the poet on the basis of his individual aesthetic sensibility. Each poet has his own taste, a personal predilection for a certain type of beauty. When he confronts a landscape, he should activate his aesthetic antenna and turn it toward the part of the landscape to which he is most attracted." A good example might be this well-known haiku of Shiki's (Beichman 53):

> I bite into a persimmon
> and a bell resounds—
> Hōryūji

Shiki's experience did involve his biting into a persimmon and simultaneously hearing the peal of a huge temple bell. It was not the bell at Hōryūji, however, but rather that of Tōdaiji, another temple in Nara. The following day he visited Hōryūji and decided that temple would suit his haiku better because of its association with famous persimmon orchards (Beichman 54).

Beyond selective realism lies the ultimate stage of Shiki's schema: *makoto*, or "poetic truthfulness." Ueda characterizes *makoto* as *shasei* directed toward the poet's internal reality: "It is based on the same principle of direct observation, except that the project to be observed is the poet's own self. The poet is to experience his inner life as simply and sincerely as he is to observe nature, and he is to describe the experience in words as simple and direct as the ancient poets— so simple and direct that they seem ordinary" (Ueda 17). An example might be Shiki's depiction of a snail, here clearly symbolic of the poet himself, supine and physically unable to raise himself more than to his elbows:

> As do I
> that snail raising its head
> to see

Shiki's advancement of *makoto* brought his literary theories full circle, admitting a full measure of subjectivity back into haiku as long as it was accompanied by truthfulness and sincerity.

Shiki began writing haiku five years after his tuberculosis first manifested itself, and from the very beginning of his professional life he was well aware that he would not enjoy a long life. If there is one topic that characterized Shiki's haiku throughout his career it would be his mortality:

> Autumn departs
> for me no gods
> no buddhas

Not surprisingly, in later years when Shiki was bedridden, more and more of his haiku dealt with such issues. Yet to a remarkable extent he was able to avoid sentimentality and self-pity. Rather, devices such as pathos, irony and gallows humor, and annoyance at his helplessness were used. Shiki referred to an out-of-season fly to emphasize his own feelings of uselessness and alienation. In the context of his illness, Shiki's "cockscombs," showy red blossoms that for him connoted cemeteries and exuberant life preceding death, have a special resonance:

What a nuisance!   Cockscomb—
a winter fly   flourishing again
dragging out its life   this autumn

Apart from preoccupation with his own fate, Shiki's topics for haiku ran the gamut from the classical to the very modern. In the present selection you will find representative echoes of Shiki's classical Chinese training and references to Japanese legends in verses such as:

Peony!   Kintoki drank
just like Yōkihi's face   from this clear spring
upon waking   and so did the bear

as well as shades of Bashō and Issa:

Spring evening—
the wifeless man
what is he reading?

Hey, toad
don't overstay your welcome
you might get trampled

On the other hand, examples of Shiki's fascination with novelties such as baseball (a particular passion of his), current events such as the Great Fire of 1900, politics, and even international affairs are everywhere evident. To take but two examples:

Under the summer moon
twenty-thousand people
homeless

In America too
raining off and on—
sound of the ocean

Shiki was a serious, focused man, so understandably there is little levity to be found in his haiku. Neither will you find anything one might call "love haiku" here—if Shiki had a serious relationship with a woman his biographers have yet to find it. Indeed, the introspective Shiki wrote very little about interpersonal relationships generally, though he did exchange haiku with his circle of disciples and friends and participated in a few *renga* (collaborative linked-verse chains, which, among his other reforms, he renamed *renku*). His main concerns for haiku were, after all, the more technical aspects of writing from nature and maintaining overall objectivity while (re)introducing elements of subjectivity and poetic truth.

An experimenter and explorer of literary boundaries, Shiki was nonetheless quite traditional in terms of haiku form. Almost without exception his haiku fit the classical Japanese 5–7–5 sound-syllable structure and feature clear caesuras (*kire*) using established cutting techniques. Only a handful of his haiku lack a season word (*kigo*).

SHIKI'S LEGACY

Such was Shiki's preeminence that his life and work profoundly influenced the haiku world, both in Japan and abroad. It would not be a great exaggeration to say that all Japanese haiku after the turn of the 20th century were infused with Shiki's teachings. His two main disciples took very different views of those principles, however, and took the genre in quite different directions.

Takahama Kyoshi adopted a conservative view of *shasei*, and in his journal *Hototogisu* and the haiku association of the same name he called for strict adherence to traditions such as syllable count and seasonality as well as restricting subject matter considered fit for haiku (dubbed *kachōfugetsu*—literally, "flower-bird-wind-moon"). Kawahigashi Hekigodō, on the other hand, believed that haiku should become more lyrical and poem-like, abandon conventions such as the 5–7–5 sound-syllable pattern as well as season words, and even avoid a single "center of interest." Many of the leading haiku poets in the early 20th century were members of the New Trend group that Hekigodō founded.

Shiki's life was congruent with the beginnings of interest in Japanese culture and literary genres in the West. Just as Shiki and his colleagues were influenced by Western aesthetics, so Anglophone scholars and orientalists were discovering and reveling in Japanese poetry. Shiki's eminence was acknowledged by the fact that translations of his works into English on a par with the classic Japanese masters, were being made within a few years of his death.

Haiku began to be written in English also about the turn of the 20Th century, mostly on the model of the classic Japanese haiku. Shiki-style *shasei* haiku were widely imitated outside Japan, which is a good thing, but the unfortunate consequences were an unthinking adoption of Japanese haiku form and the perceived necessity of using season words whose appropriateness for English-language haiku is questionable. Over the years shasei did not wear well in America and Europe, as poets fell into the rut of writing purely descriptive poems and calling them haiku. This, in turn, gave *shasei* a bad name. Haiku critics in the West often offhandedly dismiss a verse as "merely *shasei*," meaning a word photo that lacks soul.

Be this as it may, in Japan and abroad Shiki is regarded as

the most important haiku poet and innovator since Bashō. He was the first true modernist in haiku; he established a Japanese aesthetic that drew both upon poetry and painting, fused genres of writing that were completely separate in Japan into something that could properly be called "literature," and he laid the foundation for Japanese literature in the 20th century. Masaoka Shiki was the right person in the right place at the right time, and his influence continues to resonate around the globe.

Translators' Introductions

John Brandi

I first became aware of Masaoka Shiki while reading D. T. Suzuki's *Zen and Japanese Culture*, in the early 1960s. Although Suzuki presented only one haiku by Shiki, it struck a note:

> Among the grasses
> An unknown flower
> Blooming white.

As a boy I had seen that flower, high in the sunlit grasses of California's Sierra Nevada foothills. It was insignificant, nameless. It was everything. As I pressed my eye toward it, it was every bit as large as a redwood tree. Lost in its whiteness, I was inseparable from it. Fifty years later, Shiki's haiku still causes goose bumps to rise. The world pulsates. Something is flowing through it all, captivating, unexplainable.

In 1968, R.H. Blyth's four-volume *Haiku* came my way. More than three hundred of Shiki's haiku, translated by Blyth, were scattered far and wide throughout the volumes. Such a presentation did not help me get a grasp on Shiki. Instead, my attention turned to Matsuo Bashō and Kobayashi Issa, whose haiku had been collected into single books.

Decades later, when Burton Watson's *Masaoka Shiki: Selected Poems* appeared, my interest in Shiki was revived. The poems sparkled; the imagery was accessible, no frills. The seasons were there as in traditional haiku, but Shiki's approach to what was intimate within a season was unusual. In this haiku he comes to a clear sky in the month of May through sound:

> The sound of scissors
> clipping roses—
> a clear spell in May

Watson pointed out that Shiki had written over 25,000 poems in his short lifetime. But where were the originals of the poet's vast output? Was there a Shiki archive, an accessible cache somewhere in Japan? I wanted to do some research, look into Shiki's oeuvre, and begin a project where I'd work with a Japanese translator, bring some of his lesser-known haiku into English, and take a second look at a few previously translated haiku that might have misrepresented what Shiki intended.

To everything that happened next I am most appreciative. A big yes from my publisher, Dennis Maloney, at White Pine Press, who offered to publish a selection of Shiki's haiku—if my project bore fruit. Another yes from the Witter Bynner Foundation for Poetry, who agreed to support the translation venture. And a yes from each of the two people I contacted who would become vital to the plan: Noriko Kawasaki Martinez and Charles Trumbull, both living just an hour down the highway from me in Santa Fe.

Charles, a longtime student of haiku and former editor of *Modern Haiku,* was already at work gathering translations of Shiki's haiku into English (and other Western languages) into his database. The process of trying to match the English to the Japanese originals, he reminded me, was a time-consuming effort, since very few published translations included the original Japanese or the romaji. Charles had also recently returned from the Shiki Memorial Museum in Matsuyama where he was granted access to their database of Shiki's complete haiku (in Japanese), arranged by date of composition, season, and seasonal word indicator (*kigo*).

Noriko then stepped in with her expertise as a translator, and we began randomly plucking haiku from the Shiki Museum cache, deciding which might be of interest to translate, eliminating some that required too much explanation of culture or of the circumstances under which they were written. From her literal translations, Noriko and I worked back and forth with my English renderings. Over the course of one year, many afternoons were spent discussing the Japanese sensibility toward the seasons, particular cultural celebrations, details of history, specifics of the Japanese landscape, nuances of Buddhist concepts; and, of course, the multifold ramifications of the kanji.

From the onset, our desire was to compile a modest collection of Shiki's haiku to be enjoyed by a broad spectrum of readers. We felt it important to include the original Japanese and the romaji along with the English. We also wanted the poems to find their own flow, without regard for chronological or seasonal arrangement. Translation is a delicate process. Some loss is inevitable in the attempt to preserve meaning—or, in the case of haiku, to preserve the original picture. We hope we have been successful with these translations. I would like to believe that one or two haiku herein will strike a note with the reader, a gift from Shiki—beyond his critical writings, tanka, or literary prose—that ignites the imagination with a spark, and brings a glow to our otherwise troubled world.

—JB
El Rito, NM

Noriko Kawasaki Martinez

When John Brandi asked me to help him translate Shiki's work, first thing came to my mind was my childhood memory of visiting Hōryūji Temple. Shiki's haiku about eating a persimmon and hearing the temple bell is so famous that all the visitors seemed, to me, as if they were trying to listen to the sound and imagine the taste of a persimmon as Shiki had experienced.

This quick time-slip reminded me of one of the most popular questions as to how it's possible to translate haiku into any foreign language. How can we convey the senses we experience and share among Japanese people to non-Japanese people? Such doubts were replaced by excitement and curiosity when I discovered that the Shiki Museum in Matsuyama, Japan, offered a superb website. Thanks to their well-organized search system I was able to sort through Shiki's haiku by inserting a word of my choice, a season, a kigo, or a specific year in which a haiku was written, and so on.

Thus, our Shiki haiku journey began. I gave John literal translation along with grammatical and cultural explanations. Then he came up with the natural flow of words to deliver what Shiki wanted to express. Being a haiku poet himself, he did a wonderful job in achieving our goal. We also owe thanks to Charles Trumbull who generously offered us his great knowledge and help throughout our adventure.

One confession I have to reveal here is that by the time I finally finished reading more than 25,000 of Shiki's haiku, shingles and vertigo gave me good dosage of suffering. However, no comparison to what Shiki had to go through in his short life. Working on this project has given me a life-enriching experience. I feel I know Shiki as a next door neighbor, a man who, through his haiku, is still living among us.

—NKM
Santa Fe, NM

A House By Itself

Last year's dream
I wake to this year's
reality

去年の夢さめてことしのうつゝ哉

kozo no yume   samete kotoshi no   utsutsu kana

Ice has thawed
koi burst out
in small waves

氷解けぬ鯉の吹き出すさゝれ波

kōri tokenu   koi no fukidasu   sazare nami

Already spring
the snowscape still hanging
has gathered dust

雪の絵を春も掛けたる埃哉

yuki no e o   haru mo kaketaru   hokori kana

White world gone
it's about time
for the mud world

銀世界すんてそろそろ泥世界

gin sekai   sunde sorosoro   doro sekai

Dark night
I enjoy plum blossoms
with just my nose

闇の夜は鼻で探るや梅の花

yami no yo wa   hana de saguru ya   ume no hana

Chanting *namu Butsu!*
a mosquito bites
the sole of my foot

念仏や蚊にさゝれたる足の裏

nenbutsu ya   ka ni sasaretaru   ashi no ura

Lightning flash—
that laughter in the dark
belongs to a beautiful woman

稲妻や闇に美人の笑ひ聲

inazuma ya   yami ni bijin no   waraigoe

Home from the year's first play
still going about
in her festive best

初芝居見て來て曠著いまだ脱がず

hatsushibai   mite kite haregi   imada nugazu

Cherries blooming
people I remember
all far away

花咲いて思ひ出す人皆遠し

hana saite   omoidasu hito   minaōt shi

Didn't burn incense
didn't pass wind
half a spring day

香も焚かず屁もひらず春の日半日

kō mo takazu   he mo hirazu   haru no hi hannichi

The pomegranate
flowering for so long
it's almost forgotten

花石榴久しう咲いて忘られし

hana zakuro   hisashiu saite   wasurareshi

Failed to land
on the young bamboo—
a baby sparrow

若竹をおさへはづすや雀の子

wakatake o   osaehazusu ya   suzume no ko

In the haze
big islands, small islands
full sails, half sails

霞みけり大島小島真帆片帆

kasumi keri   ōshima koshima   maho kataho

After the fog clears
mountains
ten steps away

霧晴れて山は十歩の内にあり

kiri harete   yama wa jippo no   uchi ni ari

Fragrant breeze—
a temple in the green
of a thousand mountains

薫風や千山の緑寺一つ

kunpū ya　senzan no midori　tera hitotsu

Unaware
the place is famous
a man tilling a field

名所とも知らで畑打つ男哉

meisho to mo　shirade hata utsu　otoko kana

The *shōji*
shadowed bright green
　　—the banana tree

青々と障子にうつるはせを哉

aoao to　shōji ni utsuru　bashō kana

Anniversary of Bashō
alone
I eat a persimmon

芭蕉忌に参らずひとり柿を喰ふ

Bashōki ni　mairazu hitori　kaki o kuu

Tranquility—
the ocean's presence
through a hole in the *shōji*

長閑さや障子の穴に海見えて

nodokasa ya   shōji no ana ni   umi miete

An island in the lake
where no one lives
how lush the vegetation!

人住マヌ湖中ノ島ノ茂カナ

hito sumanu   kochū no shima no   shigeri kana

Peony!
just like Yōkihi's face
upon waking

楊貴妃の寐起顔なる牡丹哉

Yōkihi no   neokigao naru   botan kana

Slipping right past my eyes
a school of *ayu*
the color of water

一群の鮎目をすぎぬ水の色

hitomure no   ayu me o suginu   mizu no iro

Small garden
covered with dew
a half gallon!

一升の露をたゝふる小庭かな

isshō no   tsuyu o tatauru   saniwa kana

Sumo wrestlers
too big to view
cherry blossoms

花見には大き過たり相撲取

hanami ni wa   ōki sugitari   sumōtori

Fallen hollyhocks
trampled by festival goers—
the pageant goes on

地に落し葵踏み行く祭哉

chi ni ochishi   aoi fumiyuku   matsuri kana

These days
the hawk becomes a dove—
spring haze

鷹鳩になる此頃の朧かな

taka hato ni   naru konogoro no   oboro kana

Damned flies!
ready to swat them
they don't come near

蝿憎し打つ気になればよりつかず

hae nikushi   utsu ki ni nareba   yoritsukazu

Lone mandarin duck
how long have you been
a widower?

いつからのやもめぐらしぞをしーつ

itsu kara no   yamome gurashi zo   oshi hitotsu

Spring rain
I close my umbrella
and take a walk

春雨に傘をたゝんてあるきけり

harusame ni   kasa o tatande   aruki keri

Plum blossoms
one sprig
in my medicine bottle

一枝は薬の瓶に梅の花

hitoeda wa   kusuri no bin ni   ume no hana

Spring evening—
the wifeless man
what is he reading?

春の夜や妻なき男何を読む

haru no yo ya　tsuma naki otoko　nani o yomu

Crows sleeping
between the tree's branches
thin crescent moon

烏寐て木の間に細し三日の月

karasu nete　konoma ni hososhi　mika no tsuki

How refreshing—
the Great Buddha
his empty belly

大仏にはらわたのなき涼しさよ

Daibutsu ni   harawata no naki   suzushisa yo

The core of haiku
revealed by
a paper kimono!

俳諧のはらわた見せる紙衣かな

haikai no   harawata miseru   kamiko kana

Baby swallows
their faces all lined up
in the spring wind

春風に顔ならべけり燕の子

harukaze ni   kao narabe keri   tsubame no ko

Head down
a white lily blooming
on the boulder's edge

うつぶけに白百合さきぬ岩の鼻

utsubukeni   shirayuri   sakinu   iwa no hana

Without pause
without sound . . .
spring rain

これほどにふつて音なし春の雨
kore hodo ni　futte oto nashi　haru no ame

Still too early
the wisteria on the trellis
holds back its blooms

春早しまだ芽もふかぬ藤の棚
haru asashi　mada me mo fukanu　fuji no tana

Spring fields—
people going, people coming
what are they up to?

春の野や何に人行き人帰る

Haru no no ya   nani ni hito yuki   hito kaeru

A violet
left uneaten
by the calf

牛の子にくひ残されし菫哉

ushi no ko ni   kui nokosareshi   sumire kana

The long day—
a baby turtle inches out
from the basin

亀の子の盥這ひ出る日永哉

kame no ko no   tarai haideru   hinaga kana

A house by itself
and the moon lowering
into the grasses

家孤なり月落ちかゝる草の上

ie ko nari   tsuki ochikakaru   kusa no ue

Spring departing—
no wife, no child
in this grass hut

行春や妻も子もなき草の庵

yuku haru ya   tsuma mo ko mo naki   kusa no io

Early summer rain—
a green frog jumps up
onto the tatami

五月雨や畳に上る青蛙

samidare ya   tatami ni agaru   aogaeru

The heat!
scrawny horses
their rumps all in a row

やせ馬の尻ならべたるあつさ哉

yaseuma no　shiri narabetaru　atsusa kana

Coolness—
in front of the blacksmith's shop
willow shade

涼しさや鍛冶屋の前の柳蔭

suzushisa ya　kajiya no mae no　yanagi kage

Nap time
thunder called closer
by the sound of snoring

雷をさそふ昼寝の鼾哉

kaminari o   sasou hirune no   ibiki kana

Summer cloudburst—
green pine needles
stabbed into the sand

夕立や砂に突き立つ青松葉

yūdachi ya   suna ni tsukitatsu   aomatsuba

What heat!
a traveler catches his breath
among the weeds

炎天や草に息つく旅の人

enten ya　kusa ni iki tsuku　tabi no hito

Evening wind
after the egret lifts away
the green rice field!

夕風の鷺吹き飛ばす青田哉

yūkaze no　sagi fukitobasu　aota kana

Rainy season—
sounds of roof repair
during a lull

五月雨の晴間や屋根を直す音

samidare no   harema ya yane o   naosu oto

Hydrangeas
pale yellow in the rain
blue under the moon

紫陽花の雨に浅黄に月に青し

ajisai no   ame ni asagi ni   tsuki ni aoshi

Stifling heat—
tangled in confusion
I listen to thunder

暑くるしく乱れ心地や雷を聴く

atsukurushiku   midare gokochi ya   rai o kiku

Was going to steal
a melon, instead
I took the cool breeze

瓜盗むことも忘れて涼みかな

uri nusumu   koto mo wasurete   suzumi kana

August!
maple leaves are green
no one at the tea house

八月や人無き茶屋の青楓

hachigatsu ya　hito naki chaya no　aokaede

The fireworks stop
and then
a night of dew

花火やむあとは露けき夜也けり

hanabi yamu　ato wa tsuyukeki　yo nari keri

Full moon—
how easily I walk
through the yam field

名月やすたすたありく芋畑

meigetsu ya   suta suta ariku   imobatake

Trusting its own light?
a firefly
flying alone

おのが火をたよりか一ツ飛ぶ蛍

onoga hi o   tayori ka hitotsu   tobu hotaru

On the futon
working on haiku
rainy full-moon night

句を案す蒲團の中や月の雨

ku o anzu   futon no naka ya   tsuki no ame

Weighted by loneliness
the scarecrow—
head down

淋しさにたへてうつむく案山子哉

sabishisa ni   taete utsumuku   kakashi kana

Autumn sky
placed there
above the lake

湖の上に置きけり秋の空
mizuumi no   ue ni oki keri   aki no sora

Kintoki drank
from this clear spring
and so did the bear

金時も熊も来てのむ清水哉
Kintoki mo   kuma mo kite nomu   shimizu kana

Sailing through
the mist and finally out …
a wide open sea

漕きぬけて霞の外の海広し

koginukete   kasumi no soto no   umi hiroshi

Lost my oars
looking up from the boat
at the Milky Way

楫を絶えて舟に見る夜の天の川

kaji o taete   fune ni miru yo no   amanogawa

Autumn sky
gathered in dewdrops
blueness!

秋の空露をためたる青さかな

aki no sora   tsuyu o tametaru   aosa kana

Grapes—
a purple so deep
it's black

黒キマデニ紫深キ葡萄カナ

kuroki made ni   murasaki fukaki   budō kana

Arranging chrysanthemums
one yellow one
got left out

菊活けて黄菊一枝残りけり

kiku ikete kigiku hitoeda nokori keri

Evening prayer bell—
a ripe persimmon
thumps to the ground

晩鐘や寺の熟柿の落つる音

banshō ya tera no jukushi no otsuru oto

Bamboo fence—
garden mums on one side
wild mums on the other

竹垣や菊と野菊の裏表

takegaki ya　kiku to nogiku no　ura omote

Nobody around—
a child asleep
under the mosquito net

人もなし子一人寝たる蚊帳の中

hito mo nashi　ko hitori netaru　kaya no naka

Ripe persimmons!
the cawing crow
seems happy

柿の實やうれしさうにもなく烏

kaki no mi ya   ureshisōnimo   naku karasu

Peeling a pear—
a trickle of sweet juice
along the blade

梨むくや甘き雫の刃をたるゝ

nashi muku ya   amaki shizuku no   ha o taruru

Under the summer moon
twenty thousand people
homeless

家のなき人二万人夏の月

ie no naki   hito niman-nin   natsu no tsuki

Last of the sun—
on the gate of an empty house
a cicada crying

明家の門に蝉鳴く夕日哉

akiie no   mon ni semi naku   yūhi kana

In America too
raining off and on—
sound of the ocean

アメリカも共にしぐれん海の音

Amerika mo   tomoni shiguren   umi no oto

A sick person
asks after another sick person
  —balmy autumn day

病む人の病む人をとふ小春哉

yamu hito no   yamu hito o tou   koharu kana

Every time I look
a dragonfly on the tip
of the bamboo

いつ見ても蜻蛉一つ竹の先

itsu mitemo   tonbo hitotsu   take no saki

Abandoned house—
the aging mouse
has become a bat

鼠老いて蝙蝠となる空家哉

nezumi oite   kōmori to naru   akiya kana

Morning glory...
fading
as I paint it

朝顔ヤ絵ニカクウチニ萎レケリ

asagao ya　　e ni kaku uchi ni　　shiore keri

Spider's web
but no spider to be found
autumn wind

蜘の巣に蜘は留守也秋の風

kumo no su ni　kumo wa rusu nari　aki no kaze

My hometown—
wherever I look
mountains smile

故郷やどちらを見ても山笑ふ

furusato ya   dochira o mite mo   yama warau

Ocean and mountains
way beyond
seventeen syllables

海と山十七字に八余りけり

umi to yama   jūshichiji ni wa   amari keri

Swallow
fighting a bicycle
for the road

自転車と路を争ふ燕かな

jitensha to　michi o arasou　tsubame kana

A cedar stands tall
above the tea house—
autumn sunset

杉高く秋の夕日の茶店哉

sugi takaku　aki no yūhi no　chamise kana

Bright white moon
and red persimmons—
a monkey's dream

月白く柿赤き夜や猿の夢

tsuki shiroku　kaki akaki yo ya　saru no yume

Cockscomb—
flourishing again
this autumn

鶏頭ヤ今年ノ秋モタノモシキ

keitō ya　kotoshi no aki mo　tanomoshiki

Tree frog
hugging a pine tree
a thousand years old

千年の松をかゝへて雨蛙

sen-nen no   matsu o kakaete   amagaeru

Hey, toad
don't overstay your welcome
you might get trampled

長居してふみつぶされな蟇

nagai shite   fumitsubusare na   gamagaeru

Sunset—
after the flax harvest
a sweep of rain

日の入りや麻刈るあとの通り雨

hi no iri ya　asa karu ato no　tōri ame

Loaded with rice
a horse walking
through rice

稲つけて馬が行くなり稲の中

ine tsukete　uma ga ikunari　ine no naka

Indian summer—
colors of maples
outdo cherry blossoms

櫻にもまさる紅葉の小春かな

sakura ni mo   masaru momiji no   koharu kana

Evening darkness—
a toad spits out
the moon

宵闇や月を吐き出す蟇の口

yoiyami ya   tsuki o hakidasu   gama no kuchi

Coolness—
a waterfall tumbling
among houses

すゝしさや滝ほどばしる家のあひ

suzushisa ya   taki hotobashiru   ie no ai

As do I
that snail raising its head
to see

蝸牛の頭もたげしにも似たり

dedemushi no   atama motageshi   ni mo nitari

Autumn wind—
here we are again
still alive

秋風や生きてあひ見る汝と我

akikaze ya　ikite aimiru　nare to ware

Cemetery—
gravestones low
grasses tall

墓原や墓低くして草茂る

hakabara ya　haka hikuku shite　kusa shigeru

Under the harvest moon
clouds hurrying by
to where?

名月に飛び去る雲の行方哉

meigetsu ni   tobisaru kumo no   yukue kana

Butterflies!
the pilgrim's child
will likely lag behind

蝶蝶や順礼の子のおくれがち

chōchō ya   junrei no ko no   okuregachi

Cooling off now
no insects
at the lamp

やゝ寒み灯による虫もなかりけり

yaya samumi   hi ni yoru mushi mo   nakari keri

These leaves—
how they hold on
to the passing autumn

行く秋にしがみついたる木の葉哉

yukuaki ni   shigamitsuitaru   konoha kana

Farther and farther away
go the lanterns—
the *hototogisu*'s call

提灯の次第に遠し時鳥

chōchin no   shidai ni tōshi   hototogisu

Autumn departs
for me no gods
no buddhas

行く秋の我に神無し佛無し

yuku aki no   ware ni kami nashi   hotoke nashi

Nearing death
even louder
autumn cicadas

死にかけて尚やかましき秋の蟬

shini kakete   nao yakamashiki   aki no semi

The year's first snow—
across the sea
what mountains are they?

初雪や海を隔てゝ何處の山

hatsuyuki ya   umi o hedatete   doko no yama

Winter camellia
using all its strength
blooming red

寒椿力を入れて赤を咲く

kantsubaki　chikara o irete　aka o saku

Lone traveler
crossing the wintry field
munching an orange

旅人の蜜柑くひ行く枯野哉

tabibito no　mikan kui yuku　kareno kana

One preacher
four or five followers
  —a cold night

牧師一人信者四五人の夜寒かな

bokushi hitori   shinja shigonin no   yosamu kana

To live in the world
in a simple paper kimono
how light!

世の中を紙衣一つの輕さかな

yononaka o   kamiko hitotsu no   karusa kana

Snow on the garden
enjoyed to and from
the outhouse

庭の雪見るや厠の行き戻り

niwa no yuki   miru ya kawaya no   yukimodori

What a nuisance!
a winter fly
dragging out its life

うとましや世にながらへて冬の蠅

utomashi ya   yo ni nagaraete   fuyu no hae

Moonlit night
it's bright
behind light snow

淡雪のうしろ明るき月夜哉

awayuki no　ushiro akaruki　tsukiyo kana

A fortune told
that never came true
the year is over

占ひのつひにあたらて歳暮れぬ

uranai no　tsuini atarade　toshi kurenu

Great Buddha
his nose dripping
an icicle!

大佛の鼻水たらす氷柱哉

Daibutsu no   hanamizu tarasu   tsurara kana

Waiting for the first rooster's crow
of the New Year
a dog barks instead

初鶏の鳴くかと待てば犬吠ゆる

hatsudori no   naku ka to mateba   inu hoyuru

New Year's—
spent the whole day
thinking of nothing

元日は何も思はて暮らしけり

ganjitsu wa   nanimo omowade   kurashi keri

New Year's Day
not good, not bad—
simply human

元日は是も非もなくて衆生也

ganjitsu wa   ze mo hi mo nakute   shujō nari

Sources for the Introduction

The introductory essay is derived substantially from my earlier essays: "Crosscurrents East and West: Masaoka Shiki and the Origins of Shasei, presentation at the Haiku North America conference, August 2009, Ottawa, Ont. (reprinted in *Juxta* 2 [2016]); and "Translating Shiki: Research Note," presentation at the Haiku North America conference, September 2015, Schenectady, N.Y.

Matsuyama Municipal Shiki Memorial Museum, ed. *Collected Haiku of Shiki Sorted by Kigo*. Matsuyama, Japan: Matsuyama Municipal Shiki Memorial Museum, 1984. 25,093 haiku; in Japanese.

Janine Beichman. *Masaoki Shiki: His Life and Works*. Boston: Twayne Publishers, 1982. Reprinted by Kodansha in 1986 and by Cheng and Tsui Publishers in 2002. Biography with forty-eight haiku translations.

R. H. Blyth. *Haiku.* Tokyo: Hokuseido Press, 1949–52. Four volumes.364 haiku

———— "Shiki: The Haiku Poet," in *A History of Haiku. Volume 2: From Issa up to the Present*. Tokyo: Hokuseido Press, 1964. 77–100. Seventy-four haiku.

Harold J. Isaacson, trans. and ed. *Peonies Kana: Haiku by the Upasaka Shiki*. New York: Theatre Arts Books, 1972. 319 haiku.

Donald Keene. *The Winter Sun Shines In: A Life of Masaoka Shiki.* New York: Columbia University Press, 2013. Biography with twenty-seven haiku translations.

Masaoka Shiki. *If Someone Asks ...: Masaoka Shiki's Life and Haiku.* Translated by Shiki-Kinen Museum English Volunteers. Matsuyama, Japan: Matsuyama Municipal Shiki-kinen Museum, 2001. Biography with 116 haiku translations.

John Ruskin. *Modern Painters* (New York: Knopf, 1987; original five-volume work). This quote is on p. 365 (Volume III, page 209) in the original).

Burton Watson, trans. *Masaoka Shiki: Selected Poems.* New York: Columbia University Press, 1997. 145 haiku.

Notes on the Poems

Page 32: A scroll painting adorning a large room is customarily changed to match the new season. In this case the winter picture has been neglected.

Page 39: A *shōji* is a sliding door, room divider or window made of translucent paper stretched over a wooden frame.

Page 41: Yōkihi (Yang Kuei-fei), well-known for her beauty, was an Imperial Consort of the 8th-century Chinese Emperor Xuanzong.

Page 41: *Ayu* (*Plecoglossus altivelis*): a small fish in the salmon family, especially tasty when grilled over a fire. For many Japanese ayu brings wistful memories of summer.

Page 43: The *Aoi Matsuri*, or Hollyhock Festival, is held every May in Kyoto. Hundreds of people, dressed in Heian Period costumes adorned with hollyhocks, parade from the Imperial Palace to the ancient Kamo shrines, dedicated to the city's protection and prosperity.

Page 58: In autumn, the blaze of maples attracts thousands of viewers. Temples, shrines, gardens and tea houses are filled. In contrast, during the heat and humidity of August, the static green of the maples is bypassed.

Page 62: Sakata Kintoki: a Heian-period samurai, renowned for his strength as a warrior. A fictionalized version of Kintoki known as Kintar is a popular figure in Japan. He is a child of super-human strength, usually depicted wearing a large bib an carrying a massive ax. He is especially honored on Boy's Day.

Page 67: Throngs of people were left without homes after the devastation of Takaoka city in northwestern Toyama prefecture, usually referred to as the Great Fire of 1900.

Page 81: In Japan the lesser cuckoo (*Cuculus poliocephalus*) is known as the *hototogisu.*

The Contributors

John Brandi, poet and painter, has been a haiku practitioner for nearly forty years. Among his honors: a National Endowment for the Arts Poetry Fellowship (1979), a Witter Bynner Foundation for Poetry award to translate Mexican poetry (1985), and a White Pine Press World of Voices poetry award (2004). He gave the keynote address for the Haiku North America Conference, Ottawa (2009) and for the Punjabi Haiku Conference, India (2010). His haiku paintings have been exhibited at the New Mexico History Museum and the San Francisco Public Library. He was co-editor, with Dennis Maloney, of *The Unswept Path: Contemporary American Haiku* (2005). His recent haiku bookss include *Seeding the Cosmos* (2009), *Blue Sky Ringing* (2010), and *At it Again* (2015).

Noriko Kawasaki Martinez was born in Osaka, Japan. She majored in English Literature at the Kansai University, Osaka (1970-1973), was manager and instructor of the HANA English School, Osaka (1976-1982), and translator for the Cultural Center of La Jolla, San Diego, California (1983). After moving to Santa Fe, New Mexico, she started her own translation and tutoring business, offering her services to the Museum of International Folk Art, Santa Fe Community College, Santa Fe School for the Arts and Sciences, Santa Fe Japan Intercultural Network, and Berlitz. "What I enjoy most in my life is the 'here, now.' This is the reason why many of the haiku written by Shiki deeply touch my heart."

Charles Trumbull was the editor of *Modern Haiku*, the oldest haiku journal outside Japan, from 2006 to 2013. In 2013-14 he was Honorary Curator of the American Haiku Archives at the California State Library. In 2011, he made a solo driving trip through eleven countries in the Balkans, giving readings and meeting with haiku poets and groups. In 2014, he made a similar trip to Japan, where he presented research papers to the Hailstone Haiku Group in Kyoto, and conferred with scholars at the Museum of Haiku Literature in Tokyo and the Shiki Memorial Museum in Matsuyama. His haiku chapbooks include *Between the Chimes* (2011) and *A Five-Balloon Morning* (2013).

Special thanks to:

The Witter Bynner Foundation for Poetry,
Santa Fe, New Mexico

The Shiki Memorial Museum
Matsuyama, Japan

Companions for the Journey Series

Inspirational work by well-known writers in a small-book format designed to be carried along on your journey through life.

Volume 8
The Unswept Path: Contemporary American Haiku
Edited by John Brandi and Dennis Maloney
1-893996-38-7   220 pages

Volume 7
Lotus Moon: The Poetry of Rengetsu
Translated by John Stevens Afterword by Bonnie Myotai Treace 1-
893996-36-0   132 pages

Volume 6
A Zen Forest: Zen Sayings
Translated by Soioku Shigematsu
Preface by Gary Snyder
1-893996-30-1   120 pages

Volume 5
Back Roads to Far Towns: Basho's Travel Journal
Translated by Cid Corman
1-893996-31-X   94 pages $13.00

Volume 4
Heaven My Blanket, Earth My Pillow
Poems from Sung Dynasty China by Yang Wan-Li
Translated by Jonathan Chaves
1-893996-29-8   28 pages

Volume 3
10,000 Dawns: The Love Poems of Claire and Yvan Goll
Translated by Thomas Rain Crowe and Nan Watkins
1-893996-27-1   88 pages

Volume 2
There Is No Road: Proverbs by Antonio Machado
Translated by Mary G. Berg and Dennis Maloney
1-893996-66-2   118 pages

Volume I
Wild Ways: Zen Poems of Ikkyu
Translated by John Stevens
1-893996-65-4 152 pages